Texas Wildlife

Number One: *The Louise Lindsey Merrick Texas Environment Series*

Texas Wildlife

PHOTOGRAPHS FROM

Texas Parks & Wildlife Magazine

Introduction by DAVID BAXTER, TED L. CLARK, *and* JOHN JEFFERSON

Preface by JAMES G. TEER

 TEXAS A&M UNIVERSITY PRESS   College Station and London

Library of Congress Cataloging in Publication Data

    Texas wildlife, photographs from Texas Parks & Wildlife magazine.

    (The Louise Lindsey Merrick Texas environment series; no. 1)
    1. Zoology—Texas—Pictorial works. I. Texas Parks & Wildlife. II. Series.
QH105.T4T53   596′.09′764   77-99281
ISBN 0-89096-047-X

Manufactured in the United States of America

FIRST EDITION

For Florence Rosengren
who has meant so much to Texas

Contents

Preface

FERDINAND ROEMER, generally acclaimed as the "father of Texas geology" and a keen observer and recorder of other elements of the natural world in Texas, traveled in July, 1846, to Torrey's Trading House on the upper reaches of the Brazos to observe the country and its inhabitants. After a short sojourn there, he traveled to Austin and en route crossed the cross timbers and blackland prairies and several streams, including the Brazos, Little River, the San Gabriel, and Willis Creek. He encamped for the night at Willis Creek in Williamson County in an area not far from what came to be my family's farm. He wrote in his journal, "After a ride of several days, we came to a little brook called Willes [sic] Creek where buffaloes in great numbers were grazing. They covered the grassy prairie separated into small groups and far distant on the horizon they were visible as black specks. The number of those seen must have been not less than a thousand."

One hundred years later, as a young man then in college, I saw those buffalo. They were then bones in an Indian kitchen midden. They were there along with the bones of prairie chickens, pronghorn antelope, turkeys, and several kinds of large herons. I have seen them many times since, but only in my mind's eye, because that is the only way by which they now can be seen.

A few months after his stop at Willis Creek, Roemer traveled from San Antonio to an outpost called San Saba in Lipan Apache territory. He encamped for the night on the banks of the Llano River, and "Jim Shaw, our Indian companion, bagged a deer and a turkey and Mr. Neighbours caught a number of catfish (*Pimelodus*) each a foot long or more."

As a little older man, then working for the Texas Game, Fish and Oyster Commission in the Central Mineral Region, I became acquainted with the descendants of those same white-tailed deer and Rio Grande turkeys. They are the same animals, many generations later, that Roemer and his party ate that night on the Llano. They and canyon wrens and Inca doves and rock squirrels and javelinas and blue-winged teal and collared lizards are there in their native habitats. Now I see them and their world as often as I can, and with my optic eye, because they give me joy and pique my scientific curiosity.

So some kinds of animals are gone. And others, even more numerous than before, remain. They represent wealth of a different currency and beauty unsurpassed on canvas and chart. They lend character and form to serene and harsh environments; they have contributed to the culture and character of Texas and Texans.

Those animals that remain are here because the citizens of the state want them here. The agency appointed to oversee the job is the Texas Parks and Wildlife Department. The wardens, biologists, information and education specialists, and many others of the department have done the job. And done it well.

This book is about the art of these men and women. Their interest in art extends into the field. Some clicked the shutters to get the photographs; others made sure that the subjects were there to be photographed. They are artists all.

I want the men and women of the Texas Parks and Wildlife Department to continue to work for the natural beauty of the world. How we use the natural world is what a Higher

Being has called Stewardship and what we mortals call Conservation.

Conservation is for everyone; it is a trust that we must keep for those that follow us.

JAMES G. TEER
Wildlife and Fisheries Sciences Department
Texas A&M University

10

Acknowledgments

Texas Parks & Wildlife magazine, in which most of the photographs in this book appeared, has been the product of a number of highly creative editors, photographers, writers, and illustrators since the first issue of *Texas Game and Fish* magazine was published in December, 1942. The current format and extensive use of color photography were developed under the editorships of Wayne Tiller (1965–1970) and Neal Cook (1970–1977), to whom special credit is due.

Ilo Hiller, associate editor of *Texas Parks & Wildlife*, and LaVerne Moccia, the magazine's office manager, also deserve particular recognition for their contributions to the editing and assembly of this book, as well as for their dedicated years of service to the magazine.

At Texas A&M University, Keith A. Arnold, James R. Dixon, and David J. Schmidly of the Wildlife and Fisheries Sciences Department provided invaluable assistance in the development of this book by identifying some of the animals pictured, providing advice on common and scientific names, and supplying notes on ranges, habitats, and numbers of the wildlife.

Wildlife Management in Texas

WILD creatures always have played an important role in human affairs. Used extensively by man, they have helped to shape human thought and culture. The role of wildlife in American society is less direct today, however; people now depend more on modern agriculture and synthetics for life's essentials. Still, wildlife continues to hold a highly important and inextricable place. Evidence of this importance is the great interest in hunting and nature study and the prominence of the study of ecology as a profession. People also regard an abundance of wildlife as an indication that the environment is healthy and suitable for humans.

As the number of Texans increases, so do demands for additional outdoor recreational opportunities involving hunting, fishing, and other wildlife-oriented activities. Texas contains 262,840 square miles of land, 4,499 square miles of inland surface water, and approximately 2,100 square miles of estuaries and lagoons. The ecological regions of the state are extremely diverse, with ten regions which range from humid prairies and pine forests in the southeast and east to desert grasslands and mountains in the Trans-Pecos of the west. Some species of wildlife can be found on every square mile of these ecological regions.

Texans enjoy an abundance and diversity of wildlife unparalleled in this country. Range, farm, and forest lands, which predominate in Texas, support more than seven hundred species of wildlife. Of these, seventy-six species are classified as protected nongame, and forty-six are considered endangered and are given special protection under the Texas Nongame and Endangered Species Law.

Surveys indicate that Texas leads the nation in numbers of deer and in deer harvest. In fact, 20 percent of the nation's deer population is found in Texas.

Texas' javelina population is estimated at 125,000, or 80 percent of the nation's total.

Texas leads all states in the number of turkeys.

Texas winters 65 percent of the waterfowl in the Central Flyway.

Texas has 540 species of birds, about 100 more than are found in any other state.

And most of Texas' wildlife lives on private lands. When Texas entered the Union in 1845, one of the conditions placed upon its acceptance of statehood was that it retain title to its public lands. Much land already had been granted to homesteaders to encourage colonization, and more settlers followed. Rewards for military service during the Texas Revolution consisted of land grants which placed most of the state's land in private hands. Vast tracts of federally owned land do not exist in Texas as they do in many western states, and since the state owns less than 1 percent of the land, management of wildlife in Texas requires the cooperation of landowners.

When it comes to the state dictating land use and practices, the independent spirit of today's landowners stiffens. Owning land is an expensive proposition which requires the best possible return on the investment. A cedar brake may provide the last nesting ground in the world for a golden-cheeked warbler, but it won't fatten cattle. It doesn't help *pay* taxes, it only incurs them. A tract of brush along the Rio Grande likewise is more economical when cultivated than when left as a roosting place for white-winged doves. And coastal wetlands, to some, are best used by industry and land developers instead of as habitat for the countless creatures which occupy them, from crustaceans to whooping cranes.

There is much competition for Texas' natural habitat which is not always in the best interests of wildlife. Particularly damaging are water development projects which involve impoundment of new lakes, stream channelization, drainage of marshes and swamps, and flood prevention activities. Continuing expansion of residential areas and industrial development also are encroaching upon wildlife habitat at an alarming rate. Agricultural practices such as complete brush control and timber improvement through the growth of even-age stands tend to create biological deserts, since wildlife populations will not tolerate monotypes. They must have a variety of food and cover at all seasons of the year.

Chief hopes for sustained wildlife in Texas lie in its continued protection from illegal hunting, in wise scientific management, and, most importantly, in an increased commitment by citizen's groups and those who use the land to minimize harm to wildlife through careful planning. Texas wildlife belongs to the people of the state—not just landowners or special interest groups, but *all* Texans. The Texas Parks and Wildlife Department is the steward of these wildlife resources with the specific responsibility of managing them to the fullest and most equitable benefit of the public while preserving them for posterity.

A striking change of public attitudes is beginning to take place: people are starting to see wildlife not only as game but also as a necessary and integral part of our environment. Such attitudes and interests toward hunted and nonhunted species are being expressed through bird watching, nature study, photography, nature walks, hiking, and biking—or whatever way society has to get off the pavement and onto a trail.

During the first one hundred years of Texas' Anglo settlement, wildlife populations went from abundance to virtual depletion. The bison, bighorn sheep, and grizzly bear were either extinct or in trouble. The range of others, such as elk, pronghorn antelope, cougar, and other predatory cats, shrunk considerably. Even deer and turkey became scarce.

Now, not even halfway into the second century of Texas settlement, most species have stopped declining, and many have begun to increase.

In 1928 Texas had barely one hundred thousand white-tailed deer. A large-scale trapping and transplanting program was initiated by the Game, Fish and Oyster Commission in the mid-1940's. Since then, more than twenty-eight thousand white-tailed deer have been released in suitable habitat. Whitetails are now the state's primary big game animal, numbering well over three million. They are found in 40 percent more area than in 1945. Whitetails have an uncanny ability to adapt to civilization and have flourished to the point of overpopulation in many places. Deer will thrive given a little cover, some water, and a variety of native and domestic foods.

Only a couple of thousand pronghorn antelope were left at one time. Now, after more than five thousand pronghorns have been transplanted, they have been reestablished in most areas of suitable habitat and have multiplied tenfold. Following the transplanting of more than eleven thousand wild turkeys, this game bird is now prevalent in places which have not had turkeys since the 1930's. Texas now has four times the number of turkeys found here forty years ago. The bighorn is on its way back in West Texas. And practically everybody has heard about the whooping crane's comeback; down to only fifteen birds in 1941, sixty-nine wintered near the Aransas National Wildlife Refuge in South Texas in 1976, and another nine were reared by sandhill cranes under a foster parent program in the Rocky Mountain experimental flock.

A once sad story which we hope will have a happy ending, at least to the chapter written during our lifetime, is that of the brown pelican. Formerly numbering in the thousands in Texas, it diminished to twenty-eight adult birds in the state in 1960. By the mid-1970's, though, things were looking up, with as many as thirty-four young birds fledged in one year.

To what are these turnarounds attributable? Natural cycles? The weather? Good breeding years? Maybe some of these factors were responsible, but professional wildlife managers view the reversals, at least in part, as the products of scientific wildlife management and public understanding and acceptance of their principles.

The term *wildlife management* is often heard but seldom fully understood. It is defined as the science of making land produce sustained annual crops of wildlife for recreational use. To accomplish this task, management requires changing the characteristics and interactions of habitats, wild animal populations, and man in order to achieve a specific result.

Abundance or scarcity of wildlife is determined by the quality and availability of habitat. The existence, health, productivity, and welfare of wildlife depend on the ability of the habitat to provide all wildlife's requirements in proper quantities. As a product of the land, wildlife is, and will of necessity remain, secondary to the production of food and fiber for human consumption, but habitat is being destroyed and modified at an ever-increasing rate in an effort to satisfy the demands of our society, often with little regard to the wildlife dependent on that habitat. It is imperative that the effects of habitat destruction be determined and that programs be developed to ensure the continued production of wildlife consistent with the primary use of the land. Ignorance of the rate of habitat loss and lack of means for the prevention of such loss are among the major problems facing those interested in preserving wildlife.

In man's attempts to alter the environment to suit his purposes, he has drastically modified the previously ecologically balanced effects of disease, parasites, and predators and has created the grim consequences of pollution. As wildlife is crowded into ever-shrinking habitats, and as recreational demands on wildlife grow, the removal of wildlife by disease, parasites, pollution, and predators will assume greater importance. The effects on wildlife of these decimating factors are, in most cases, subtle and ecologically complicated. These factors must be identified, and programs must be developed to contain their harmful effects within acceptable limits. This is the task of the wildlife manager.

Before wildlife can be managed, the nature of the problem must be fully and completely understood. To the wildlife biologist this understanding includes a knowledge of the wildlife species he is managing, their relative number and distribution, the habitat available to support them, their productivity, their mortality (both natural and by hunting), their movements, and, most importantly and perplexingly, how they affect and are affected by all other species in their environment. From an evaluation of all these factors a management plan is formulated which will serve the best interests of the public through the sustained use of the wildlife resource.

Most management techniques have evolved in Texas during the last fifty years or so. The first game wardens were appointed in 1919, with only six of them to cover the entire state. During the late 1920's and early 1930's the public and lawmakers began to see the need for wildlife management. The Pittman-Robertson Act provided federal aid for wildlife restoration, and in 1938 Texas became the first state to take advantage of it. Twelve biologists were employed by the old Texas Game, Fish and Oyster Commission, and research was begun. One of their first assignments was to assess the status of the state's major game resources. This assessment was completed and published in 1945 as *Principal Game Birds and Mammals of Texas: Their Distribution and Management.*

In 1943 the legislature placed the Trans-Pecos counties of far West Texas under the regulatory authority of the Texas Game and Fish Commission. That was the beginning of hunting and fishing regulations as set by a commission instead of the legislature. Subsequent legislation placed additional counties under regulatory authority for some or all species. The Texas Parks and Wildlife Commission, as the governing board of the state's conservation agency is currently called, now sets regulations for all but a few of the state's 254 counties.

Early wildlife research and management was organized on a regional basis instead of statewide. Attempts at comprehensive species management began in 1947 with research projects on white-winged doves and waterfowl. These projects, too, were somewhat regional, since whitewings were largely restricted to the Rio Grande Valley and waterfowl hunting was concentrated along the coast.

The first statewide species-oriented project focused on the mourning dove. This project was initiated in 1966 to manage the species within Texas. The ultimate goal of the dove project is to define the various segments of the population and measure the environmental factors affecting those segments. The dove project has shown a need for a statewide approach to many game management problems. A piecemeal approach on a local basis could be inadequate.

Species management, as it has been applied by the Texas Parks and Wildlife Department, combines research and management efforts for a particular bird or animal in every area of the state and is coordinated under the direction of a single leader. Specific needs of a species within a particular area are handled locally on a statewide priority basis.

The principal management tool available to a state conservation agency is protection through the regulated taking of wildlife. Any bird or animal not designated as game usually is either completely protected, as are songbirds, or completely unprotected, as are rabbits. This tool traditionally has been applied by county. Unfortunately, using county lines to define the boundaries of a management unit probably is more socially and politically influenced than biologically precise. Neither wildlife nor its problems stop at county lines, and some situations do not affect a whole county, although current regulations usually apply as if they did.

Meaningful species management units will be developed to put into effect statewide species management. Satellite and computer-assisted statewide habitat mapping programs are under way. Valuable habitat information already has been gathered by LANDSAT, the common designation for the Earth Resources Technological Satellite. Circling the earth every 103 minutes, each of two such satellites scans the terrain below and relays information which is stored on computer tape. Through an intricate conversion system, biologists are able to map habitat composition throughout the state. The various types, amounts, and distribution of vegetation indicated on the maps are keys to wildlife abundance in a given area, and the maps will be valuable to future management.

Information derived from a satellite five hundred miles above the earth, though, has not replaced the man on the ground when it comes to making wildlife population surveys. In order to determine populations, biologists use a variety of methods designed to provide not only numbers but also the structure of the populations. Every effort is made to obtain the most accurate surveys possible by using biologists on foot, motorized ground census taking equipment, and helicopters and fixed-wing aircraft. The same census lines are surveyed each year to indicate density and trends in population. Population changes over a period of years can be detected in order to make corrections.

Game populations obviously are affected by hunting pressure, and the extent of the effect is of vital interest to wildlife managers. Consequently, game harvest surveys are conducted to measure the influence of recreational hunting. Harvest data are the easiest and most reliable to collect. Population density, reproduction, and natural mortality, on the other hand, are difficult and expensive to determine. Well-designed harvest surveys also determine sex and age composition of the animals being harvested. This information warns wildlife managers when a particular sex or age class is being overused so that harvest regulations can be adjusted to reduce the pressure.

Harvest surveys also provide data on the timing of the harvest. This information is used in management decisions designed to redirect the harvest and modify the take by sex, age, or segment of the population.

Another management tool which has been highly successful in Texas is the stocking or restocking of animals into habitats capable of supporting larger populations of particular species. One of the more successful restocking efforts has been that for the eastern turkey. It once roamed East Texas forests from the Trinity River to the Louisiana border in plentiful numbers, but by the early 1900's this game bird had all but been eliminated from its native range as land clearing and loss of hardwood trees decreased its range and as illegal hunting also took its toll.

Biologists were confident that turkeys could be reestablished in East Texas with proper protection. Native Rio Grande turkeys which were available from southern and western Texas were trapped and transplanted, but to no avail. The damp forests and bottomlands proved unsuitable for the Rio Grande strain. These transplants from the more arid parts of Texas were unsuccessful in nesting and poult production.

Eastern turkey brood stock was ultimately obtained through cooperation with southeastern states, and a propagation program was begun. More than eight hundred turkeys have been released since 1971, and populations have increased to the point that a spring season on gobblers was permitted in portions of two counties in 1976—the first legal hunting of eastern turkeys in fifty years.

Turkeys are stocked only under strict procedures designed to provide the best chances for survival. Landowners must have a minimum of eight thousand acres in one block and must agree to prohibit turkey hunting for up to five breeding seasons, with an option for five additional seasons.

Although habitat modifications have been detrimental to some species, changes in land use have made possible the successful stocking of other species. For example, as the coastal prairies were converted from grasslands to rice farms, much bobwhite quail habitat was destroyed. But ring-necked pheasants, unlike quail, require comparatively little woody cover and thrive on open land. A detailed ecological study was made of the game-deficient areas before it was determined that pheasants would be suitable replacements for bobwhites.

Originally stocked in Matagorda and Jackson counties in 1964, the birds adapted well in some areas. Subsequent stocking in the rice farming areas of Liberty, Jefferson, and Matagorda counties has proven so successful that hunting now is permitted for the cock pheasants not needed for reproduction. It is hoped that the pheasant will be able to maintain itself and become a new game bird in areas no longer as well suited for native species.

But things have not gone as well for the bighorn sheep. A restocking program for the sheep has been marked by as many setbacks as successes. Desert bighorn sheep once were plentiful in the southwestern United States, including West Texas and New Mexico. They now are found in quantity only in the Mexican states of Sonora and Baja California. The coming of the railroad in the 1800's brought about the decline of the species. Its smoothly curved, majestically curling horns made it one of the most highly sought trophies on the continent. Trophy and market hunting, combined with disease, ultimately brought it to the brink of extinction.

By 1941 what had been a herd of 1,500 sheep in West Texas numbered only 150. The last sighting of a native bighorn in the wild took place in the Sierra Diablo Mountains north of Van Horn in 1960.

In an effort to restore the sheep, brood stock was trapped in Arizona and brought to Texas in the late 1950's. The herds grew well for several years, and in 1970, twenty adult sheep were released in the wild in the Black Gap Wildlife Management Area. Then disease and predation began taking their toll. During the mid-1970's, mountain lions annihilated the annual lamb crops.

Recent trapping in Mexico provided additional brood stock, and cooperation from private ranching interests has provided a new boost to bighorn management. Under an agreement which guarantees protection and insures the state's rights to the sheep, a private ranch has constructed a mountain lion–proof fence around a large pasture. The sheep have been placed inside the enclosure with the hope that they will increase and be stocked in a suitable habitat.

Before their release the sheep are kept under observation for nearly a year at the Parks and Wildlife Department's Black Gap Wildlife Management Area. Much of the department's research is conducted on such wildlife management areas, thirteen of which are located throughout the state. Various studies done on such areas include food plot comparisons, competition between game and domestic livestock, habitat improvement, parasite and disease control, nesting conditions, trapping and banding activities, and nutritional programs. Several studies have been conducted in cooperation with universities, including Texas A&M University. Limited hunting is permitted on some of the wildlife management areas to assist in gathering data for management research. All big game and some of the small-game animals and birds harvested are weighed and measured, and various other data are obtained.

In addition to helping gather data, sport hunting controls populations and provides recreation. Cougars, wolves, and other natural predators no longer keep populations in balance as they once did. Less efficient predators such as human hunters and domestic dogs and cats inhibit population growth to an extent, with nature doing the rest. During a prolonged drought, severe winter, or combination of the two the number of birds or animals is determined by the survival of the individuals best able to compete for food. Regulated hunting provides a much more humane approach to population problems and less wasteful use of wildlife.

In return for the recreation which hunters receive, hunters' dollars have provided the funds for wildlife management. From the days of Teddy Roosevelt and John J. Audubon—both avid hunters—it has been the hunters who provided both the impetus and the money for wildlife programs. More than five hundred million dollars in federal excise taxes on firearms and ammunition and one hundred million dollars from hunting license sales go to wildlife management nationally each year. And sportsmen's organizations such as Ducks Unlimited have spent twenty-two million dollars since 1972 for preservation of Canadian marshlands where more than three-fourths of our ducks and geese are produced. Sportsmen's dollars fund an imposing number of projects at the local, state, and federal levels. And revenues from sport hunting have helped preserve wildlife habitats for the benefit of nongame as well as game animals.

Since there are more demands placed on game animals through hunting pressure, and more management money available through license fees and federal excise taxes on guns and ammunition, much of this text concerns game management. But the Texas Parks and Wildlife Department works for conservation of *all* wildlife resources, as anyone knows who reads *Texas Parks & Wildlife* magazine or who scans the pages of this book. Although some of the principles of wildlife management discussed here are couched in terms of game management, most of the principles themselves apply to nongame species as well.

The Texas Parks and Wildlife Department initiated a comprehensive nongame program in 1970. The goal of this program is to maintain populations of nongame wildlife for their functional value in the ecosystem as well as for their aesthetic, educational, and scientific values. In the beginning the nongame program was funded by the same sources as all other wildlife activities—the hunter. However, realizing that nongame wildlife is the responsibility of all citizens and not just sportsmen, the Texas Legislature in 1973 began to fund the department's nongame activities with a specific appropriation from general revenue sources. Although money for this program has been limited, the department has made notable advancements in nongame wildlife management.

Principal activities of the nongame program include field research and determination of the population status of specific nongame species. Other activities involve response to requests for information from the public and from local, state, and federal agencies; review of the status of species proposed for protection under state and federal statutes; and response to problems that pose an immediate threat to the existence of nongame species.

Investigations conducted under the nongame program led to the establishment of lists of endangered and protected nongame species, the latter equivalent to the federal threatened category of wildlife. Designation as an endangered or protected nongame species brings that species under full protection of the Parks and Wildlife Department and provides penalties for illegal taking which are more severe than those for illegal taking of games species under the department's protection.

It is unfortunate that the coalition between sport hunting and game management interests did not form sooner in this country. Had such an alliance existed fifty or one hundred years earlier, we might still have the passenger pigeon and perhaps could see a black-footed ferret now and then. There is little doubt population counts and harvest surveys of the bison would have signaled the need for protective regulations. Surely some species would have suffered from the advances of civilization just as some are suffering now. But had there been capacity for assessing and treating the problem sooner, the endangered species list might be shorter and more realistic today.

Since the advent of modern game management, which permits hunting based on the existence of biological surpluses of wildlife, no game species in North America has been severely depleted by sport hunting, and many species have been brought from scarcity to abundance. Wildlife's greatest threat is not from controlled hunting, but from uncontrolled use and abuse of the environment.

Many segments of society have differing views on the proper use of wildlife. Each, in its own way, professes to have as one of its chief goals the conservation of wildlife resources for future generations. With that common denominator, we hope all those who would turn the pages of this book will join in the common task of teaching others of the need for altering economic activities so there always will be a place for Texas wildlife.

DAVID BAXTER
TED L. CLARK
JOHN JEFFERSON
Texas Parks and Wildlife Department

PLATES

Red Fox

Gray Fox

Gray Fox

Gray Wolf

Red Wolf

Coyotes

Bobcat

Mountain Lion

Jaguar

Raccoon

Raccoon

Raccoon

Young Ringtails

36

Ringtail

Badger

Western Hog-nosed Skunk

Striped Skunk

Cottontail

Black-tailed Jack Rabbit

Black-tailed Jack Rabbit

Southern Flying Squirrel

Texas Antelope Ground Squirrel

Fox Squirrel

Fox Squirrel

Fox Squirrel

Porcupine

Beaver

Black-tailed Prairie Dog

Javelinas

Javelinas

Javelinas

Wild Hog

Nine-banded Armadillo

Nine-banded Armadillo

Short-tailed Shrew

Virginia Opossum

Mule Deer

Mule Deer

White-tailed Deer

White-tailed Deer Fawns

White-tailed Deer Fawn

White-tailed Deer

Young White-tailed Deer

White-tailed Deer

Bighorn Sheep

Bighorn Sheep

Elk

Pronghorns

Overleaf: Pronghorns

Great Egret

Snowy Egret

74

Roseate Spoonbill

Whooping Crane

Louisiana Heron

Great Blue Heron

Yellow-crowned Night Herons

Roseate Spoonbill

Great Egret

Reddish Egret

Snowy Egret

82

Black-crowned Night Heron

Louisiana Heron

Young White-faced Ibis

Ring-billed Gull

Laughing Gulls

Killdeer

Laughing Gull

Long-billed Curlew

Brown Pelican

Brown Pelican

White Pelicans

Anhinga

Mallards

Mallards

Black-bellied Whistling Ducks

Canada Geese

Snow Geese

98

Snow and Blue Geese

Pintails

99

Blue-winged Teal

Pintails

Lesser Scaup

White-fronted Goose

Redheads

Canada Geese

American Robins

White-crowned Sparrow

Male Cardinal

Female Cardinal

Mockingbird

Mockingbirds

Townsend's Warbler

Northern Parula

Virginia's Warbler

Black-and-White Warbler

Lichtenstein's Oriole

Western Meadowlark

Mountain Bluebird

Golden-cheeked Warbler

Scrub Jay

Green Jay

Blue Jay

Mexican Jay

Steller's Jay

Young Blue Jay

Scrub Jay

Green Jay

Vermilion Flycatcher

Western Kingbirds

Turkey Vulture

Green Violet-ear

Green Kingfisher

Pileated Woodpeckers

Young Pileated Woodpecker

Pileated Woodpecker

Red-bellied Woodpecker

Red-headed Woodpecker

Common Flicker

Screech Owl

Great Horned Owl

Young Screech Owl

Burrowing Owl

American Kestrel

Red-tailed Hawk

Hook-billed Kite

Southern Bald Eagle

Roadrunner

Roadrunner

Harlequin Quail

Bobwhite

Bobwhite

Gambel's Quail

140

Chachalaca

Attwater's Greater Prairie Chicken

White-winged Dove

145

Attwater's Greater Prairie Chicken

White-winged Dove

Mourning Dove

146

Mourning Doves

Inca Dove

Band-tailed Pigeon

Common Ground Dove

White-winged Dove

Wild Turkey

Wild Turkey

151

Wild Turkeys

Wild Turkey

Five-lined Skinks

Green Anole

Slender Glass Lizard

Greater Earless Lizard

Ground Skink

Collared Lizard

Reticulated Collared Lizard

Tree Lizard

Green Anole

Small-mouthed Salamander

Whiptail

Marbled Salamander

Mole Salamander

American Alligators

American Alligator

Speckled Kingsnake

Blotched Water Snake

Western Mud Snake

Blotched Water Snake

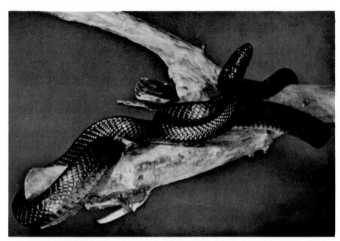

Texas Indigo Snake

Bullsnake

Trans-Pecos Rat Snake

Diamondback Water Snake

Coachwhip

Eastern Hognosed Snakes

Rough Green Snake

Black-necked Garter Snake

Texas Coral Snake

Western Cottonmouth

Prairie Kingsnake

Copperhead

Prairie Rattlesnake

Western Diamondback Rattlesnake

Northern Gray Tree Frog

Upland Chorus Frog

Texas Cliff Frog

Southern Leopard Frog

Giant Toad

Gulf Coast Toad

Green Tree Frog

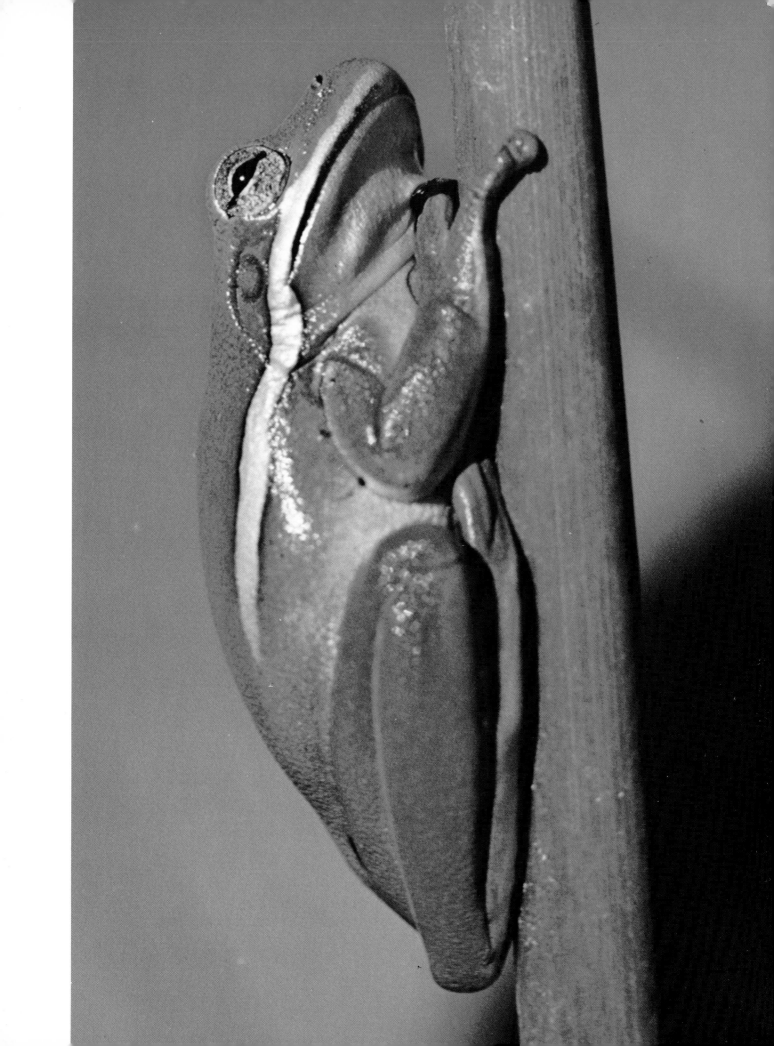

Gulf Coast Toad

Spiny Softshell Turtle

Red-eared Turtle

Common Snapping Turtle

Eastern Box Turtle

Western Box Turtle

River Cooter

Notes and Photographic Credits

Bobcat. *Lynx rufus*. Frontispiece and page 29 photographs by Reagan Bradshaw; page 30 photograph by Jim Whitcomb. Found statewide, with a preference for rocky canyons or outcrops.

Red fox. *Vulpes vulpes*. Page 22 photograph by Leroy Williamson. Primarily an inhabitant of eastern Texas woodlands, but has been introduced into central Texas for sport.

Gray fox. *Urocyon cinereoargenteus*. Pages 23 and 24 photographs by Karl H. Maslowski; page 25 photograph by Jim Whitcomb. An inhabitant of wooded areas throughout Texas.

Gray wolf. *Canis lupus*. Page 26 photograph by Phil A. Dotson. Endangered; formerly common in the grasslands of Texas, where it preyed upon buffalo, it is today rarely seen in the state except for a few individuals that have crossed from Mexico into Trans-Pecos Texas.

Red wolf. *Canis rufus*. Page 26 photograph by Perry Shankle, Jr.; page 27 photograph by Reagan Bradshaw. An endangered species. Restricted to the upper Gulf Coast counties.

Coyote. *Canis latrans*. Page 28 *above*, photograph by Martin T. Fulfer; *below*, photograph by Perry Shankle, Jr. Found statewide; common.

Mountain lion (cougar; puma). *Felis concolor*. Page 31 photograph by Perry Shankle, Jr. Found in western and southern Texas. Uncommon except in the most remote areas.

Jaguar. *Felis onca*. Page 31 photograph by Carlos Rivero-Blanco. Occurs in South Texas, but is extremely rare.

Raccoon. *Procyon lotor*. Page 32 photograph by Martin T. Fulfer; page 33 photograph by Ed Dutch; page 34 photograph by Perry Shankle, Jr. Common throughout the state.

Ringtail. *Bassariscus astutus*. Pages 35 and 36 photographs by John Suhrstedt; page 37 photograph by Leroy Williamson. Common in rocky areas of western and central Texas.

Badger. *Taxidea taxus*. Page 38 photograph by Martin T. Fulfer. Occurs over all but extreme eastern Texas.

Western hog-nosed skunk. *Conepatus mesoleucus*. Page 38 photograph by Perry Shankle, Jr. Most common in the Edwards Plateau and Trans-Pecos regions of Texas.

Striped skunk. *Mephitis mephitis*. Page 39 photograph by Martin T. Fulfer. Common throughout the state.

Cottontail. *Sylvilagus* sp. Page 40 photograph by Karl H. Maslowski; page 41 photograph by Jim Whitcomb. Distributed statewide.

Black-tailed jack rabbit (California jack rabbit). *Lepus californicus*. Page 42 photograph by Frank Aguilar; page 43 photograph by Bill Reaves. Common over all but extreme eastern Texas.

Southern flying squirrel. *Glaucomys volans*. Page 44 photograph by Black Hawk Films, Inc. Inhabits the forests of eastern Texas.

Texas antelope ground squirrel. *Ammospermophilus interpres*. Page 44 photograph by Jim Whitcomb. Characteristic of the desert regions of western Texas.

Fox squirrel. *Sciurus niger*. Page 45 photograph by Bill Reaves; pages 46 and 47 photographs by Jim Whitcomb. Important small game mammal in eastern and central Texas.

Porcupine. *Erethizon dorsatum*. Page 48 photograph by Neal Cook. Common in the Trans-Pecos, Edwards Plateau, and High Plains regions of the state.

Beaver. *Castor canadensis*. Page 48 photograph by Perry Shankle, Jr. Known from all major rivers in eastern and southern Texas.

Black-tailed prairie dog. *Cynomys ludovicianus*. Page 49 photograph by Jim Whitcomb. Occurs in colonies or "towns" in the western half of Texas.

Javelina (collared peccary). *Tayassu tajacu*. Page 50 *above* and page 51, photographs by Walter Elling; page 50 *below*, photograph by Max Traweek; page 52 *above*, photograph by Ed Dutch; page 52 *below*, photograph by Jim Whitcomb. Occurs in western Texas and the brush country south of San Antonio.

Wild hog (feral pig; razorback). *Sus scrofa*. Page 53 photograph by Jim Whitcomb. Its ancestors were once domestic pigs.

Nine-banded armadillo. *Dasypus novemcinctus*. Page 54

photograph by Leroy Williamson; page 55 photograph by Jim Whitcomb. Common in eastern, central, and southern Texas.

Short-tailed shrew. *Blarina brevicauda*. Page 56 photograph by Martin T. Fulfer. Rare; occurs in extreme eastern Texas. May be easily confused with the least shrew.

Virginia opossum. *Didelphis virginiana*. Page 57 photograph by John Dyes. Common throughout most of the state.

White-tailed deer. *Odocoileus virginianus*. Page 58 photograph by Leroy Williamson; page 60 *above*, photograph by Frank Aguilar; page 60 *below*, photograph by Bill Wilson; pages 61 and 64 photographs by Perry Shankle, Jr.; page 62 photograph by Jim Whitcomb; page 63 photograph by Bill Reaves; page 65 photograph by Ed Dutch. Common in brushy or wooded country throughout Texas; the state's primary big game species.

Mule deer. *Odocoileus hemionus*. Page 59 *above*, photograph by Bill Reaves; *below*, photograph by Reagan Bradshaw. Common in the Trans-Pecos and High Plains areas of the state.

Bighorn sheep (desert bighorn; mountain sheep). *Ovis canadensis*. Pages 66–69 photographs by Reagan Bradshaw. Native sheep, Texas bighorns, have been extirpated, but desert bighorns have recently been reintroduced into the Trans-Pecos region.

Elk (wapiti). *Cervus elaphus*. Page 70 *above*, photograph by Leroy Williamson; *below*, photograph by Glen Mills. Native elk, Merriam's elk (*Cervus merriami*), are extinct, but individuals of *C. elaphus* have been reintroduced into the Guadalupe Mountains of the Trans-Pecos region.

Pronghorn. *Antilocapra americana*. Page 71 *above*, photograph by Leroy Williamson; *below*, photograph by Reagan Bradshaw; pages 72–73 photograph by Martin T. Fulfer. Once almost extinct, its numbers have increased in the Trans-Pecos, the Permian Basin, and the Panhandle.

Great egret (common egret). *Casmerodius albus*. Page 74 photograph by Bill Duncan; page 82 photograph by C. J. Simmons. Largest of the white egrets; breeds in eastern and southern Texas.

Snowy egret. *Egretta thula*. Page 74 photograph by Frank Aguilar; page 75 photograph by Paul Hope; page 82 photograph by Bill Reaves. Once rare because it was hunted for its plumes.

Roseate spoonbill. *Ajaia ajaja*. Page 76 photograph by Norm Arnold; pages 80 and 81 photographs by Bill Reaves. Once threatened by plume hunters.

Whooping crane. *Grus americana*. Page 77 photograph by Bill Reaves. Endangered; winters along the central Texas Gulf coast.

Louisiana heron (tricolored heron). *Hydranassa tricolor*. Pages 77 and 83 photographs by Bill Reaves. One of the most common herons on the Gulf Coast.

Great blue heron. *Ardea herodias*. Page 78 photograph by Bill Reaves. Occurs statewide; largest of the Texas herons and egrets.

Yellow-crowned night heron. *Nycticorax violacea*. Page 79 photograph by John Tveten. An inland nester that forms small colonies.

Reddish egret. *Hydranassa rufescens*. Page 82 photograph by Jim Whitcomb. Generally restricted to the Gulf Coast.

Black-crowned night heron. *Nycticorax nycticorax*. Page 83 photograph by Frank Aguilar. Winters in Texas.

White-faced ibis. *Plegadis chihi*. Page 83 photograph (immature bird) by Neal Cook. Threatened; susceptible to pesticides.

Ring-billed gull. *Larus delawarensis*. Page 84 photograph by John Suhrstedt. Generally a winter visitor to the coast and inland lakes.

Laughing gull. *Larus atricilla*. Page 85 photograph by Bill Reaves; page 87 photograph by Tim Leifeste. Generally a coastal bird; abundant.

Killdeer. *Charadrius vociferus*. Page 86 photograph by Jim Whitcomb. Common statewide.

Long-billed curlew. *Numenius americanus*. Page 88 photograph by Reagan Bradshaw; page 89 photograph by Jim Whitcomb. A common winter visitor to coastal marshes and prairies.

Brown pelican. *Pelicanus occidentalis*. Pages 90 and 91 photographs by Reagan Bradshaw. Endangered; formerly common on the Gulf Coast.

White pelican. *Pelicanus erythrorhynchos*. Page 92 photograph by Neal Cook. Found in large flocks along the Gulf Coast in winter.

Anhinga (water turkey; snakebird). *Anhinga anhinga*. Page 93 photograph by Perry Shankle, Jr. Often seen submerged with only the head and neck above water.

Mallard. *Anas platyrhynchos*. Page 94 photographs by Leroy Williamson; pages 95 and 96 photographs by Bill Reaves. A popular duck with hunters.

Black-bellied whistling duck (black-bellied tree duck). *Dendrocygna autumnalis*. Page 97 photograph by Ed Dutch. Generally restricted to South Texas and the coastal prairies.

Canada goose. *Branta canadensis*. Pages 98 and 101 photographs by Leroy Williamson. The common "dark" goose of Texas hunters.

Snow goose and blue goose. *Chen caerulescens*. Page 98 photograph by Jim Whitcomb; page 99 photograph by Leroy Williamson. These geese reach the state in huge numbers. They are different color phases of the same species.

Pintail. *Anas acuta*. Pages 99 and 100 photographs by Bill Reaves. One of the most abundant ducks wintering in Texas.

Blue-winged teal. *Anas discors*. Page 100 photograph by Jim Whitcomb. A fast-flying early migrant.

Lesser scaup. *Aythya affinis*. Page 100 photograph by Bill Reaves. Diving birds often seen in large rafts.

White-fronted goose. *Anser albifrons*. Page 101 photograph by Reagan Bradshaw. Called "speckle-belly" by Texas hunters.

Redhead. *Aythya americana*. Page 101 photograph by Rex Schmidt. Texas is the major wintering grounds for this species.

American robin. *Turdus migratorius*. Page 102 photograph by Perry Shankle, Jr. Breeds in Texas; also winters in the state in the millions.

White-crowned sparrow. *Zonotrichia leucophrys*. Page 103 photograph by Martin T. Fulfer. A common winter visitor.

Cardinal. *Cardinalis cardinalis*. Page 104 photograph (male) by Martin T. Fulfer; page 105 photograph (female) by Bill Reaves. A common resident of Texas.

Mockingbird. *Mimus polyglottos*. Page 106 photograph by Martin T. Fulfer; page 107 photograph by Reagan Bradshaw. The state bird of Texas.

Townsend's warbler. *Dendroica townsendi*. Page 108 photograph by John Tveten. A rare migrant in West Texas.

Northern parula (parula warbler). *Parula americana*. Page 108 photograph by John Tveten. A common summer resident in the river bottoms of East Texas.

Virginia's warbler. *Vermivora virginiae*. Page 109 photograph by John Tveten. Nests only in the Guadalupe Mountains in West Texas.

Black-and-white warbler. *Mniotilta varia*. Page 109 photograph by John Tveten. An early spring migrant in the state.

Lichtenstein's oriole. *Icterus gularis*. Page 110 photograph by Bill Reaves. Occurs in South Texas, but is rare.

Western meadowlark. *Sturnella neglecta*. Page 111 photograph by Jim Whitcomb. Widespread in grasslands.

Mountain bluebird. *Sialia currucoides*. Page 112 photograph by Jim Whitcomb. Found in West Texas in winter.

Golden-cheeked warbler. *Dendroica chrysoparia*. Page 113 photograph by L. G. "Red" Adams and Lew V. Adams. Nests only in mature stands of ash juniper in central Texas.

Scrub jay. *Aphelocoma coerulescens*. Page 114 photograph by John Tveten; page 116 photograph by Reagan Bradshaw. A common resident of central and western Texas.

Green jay. *Cyanocorax yncas*. Page 114 photograph by John Tveten; page 117 photograph by Reagan Bradshaw. A South Texas specialty.

Blue jay. *Cyanocitta cristata*. Pages 114 and 115 photographs by John Tveten. A common resident of the eastern half of the state.

Mexican jay. *Aphelocoma ultramarina*. Page 115 photograph by John Tveten. Generally restricted to the Big Bend country.

Steller's jay. *Cyanocitta stelleri*. Page 115 photograph by John Tveten. Breeds in the Guadalupe and Davis mountains of West Texas.

Vermilion flycatcher. *Pyrocephalus rubinus*. Page 118 photograph by Perry Shankle, Jr. Usually found in arid regions of the state.

Eastern kingbird. *Tyrannus tyrannus*. Page 119 photograph by Neal Cook. A ferocious defender of its nest.

Western kingbird. *Tyrannus verticalis*. Page 120 photograph by Leroy Williamson. Common in the western half of the state.

Turkey vulture. *Cathartes aura*. Page 121 photograph by Perry Shankle, Jr. Ranges statewide; a common carrion feeder along Texas highways.

Green violet-ear. *Colibri thalassinus*. Page 122 photograph by John Suhrstedt. A rare hummingbird visitor from Mexico.

Green kingfisher. *Chloroceryle americana*. Page 123 photograph by Dan Klepper. Found in South Texas and the southern part of the Edwards Plateau.

Pileated woodpecker. *Dryocopus pileatus*. Pages 124 and 125 photographs by Robert C. White. Often confused with the ivory-billed woodpecker.

Red-bellied woodpecker. *Melanerpes carolinus*. Page 126 photograph by Bill Reaves. A common bird of eastern woodlands.

Red-headed woodpecker. *Melanerpes erythrocephalus*. Page 126 photograph by John Suhrstedt. Becoming scarce in much of its range.

Common flicker (yellow-shafted flicker). *Colaptes auratus*. Page 127 photograph by Gary Shackleford. A common winter visitor; a "ground woodpecker."

Screech owl. *Otus asio*. Pages 128 and 129 photographs by Ed Dutch. The common small "eared" owl in the state.

Great horned owl. *Bubo virginianus*. Page 128 photograph by Ed Dutch. Found statewide; the largest resident owl.

Burrowing owl. *Athene cunicularia*. Page 130 photograph by Martin T. Fulfer. Closely associated with prairie dog colonies.

Barn owl. *Tyto alba*. Page 131 photograph by John Tveten. The "monkey-faced" owl; occurs statewide.

American kestrel. *Falco sparverius*. Page 132 photograph by Ed Dutch. Once known as the sparrow hawk.

Red-tailed hawk. *Buteo jamaicensis*. Page 133 photograph by Bill Reaves. The common hawk breeding in the open country of eastern and central Texas.

Hook-billed kite. *Chondrohierax uncinatus*. Page 134 photograph by Ed Dutch. A rare breeder in South Texas.

Southern bald eagle. *Haliaeetus leucocephalus leucocephalus*. Page 135 photograph by Martin T. Fulfer. Endangered; breeds in Texas.

Roadrunner (chaparral cock; paisano). *Geococcyx californianus*. Page 136 photograph by Bill Reaves; page 137 photograph by John Tveten. This large ground cuckoo eats snakes and lizards.

Harlequin quail (Montezuma's quail; fool's quail; Mearns's quail). *Cyrtonyx montezumae mearnsi*. Page 138 photograph by Pat O'Brien. Rare; restricted to the Davis Mountains and the western part of the Edwards Plateau.

Bobwhite. *Colinus virginianus*. Page 138 *above*, photograph by Leroy Williamson; *below*, photograph by Ed Dutch; page 139 photograph by Perry Shankle, Jr. The name of this quail is derived from the sound of its call notes.

Gambel's quail. *Lophortyx gambelii*. Page 140 photograph by Gary R. Zahm. Confined to areas along the Rio Grande.

Scaled quail (blue quail). *Callipepla squamata*. Page 141 photograph by Bill Reaves. An inhabitant of dry country.

Chachalaca. *Ortalis vetula*. Page 142 photograph by John Suhrstedt; page 143 photograph by John Tveten. Found in bottomland habitats along the Rio Grande in South Texas.

Attwater's greater prairie chicken. *Tympanuchus cupido*. Pages 144–145 photographs by John Tveten. An endangered species of the Texas coastal prairie.

White-winged dove. *Zenaida asiatica*. Page 145 photograph by Bill Reaves; pages 146 and 149 photographs by Martin T. Fulfer. A highly popular game bird of South Texas and Trans-Pecos brushlands.

Mourning dove. *Zenaida macroura*. Pages 146 and 147 photographs by Bill Reaves. The most hunted game bird in Texas; found statewide.

Inca dove (scaled dove). *Scardafella inca*. Page 148 photograph by Ed Dutch. Occurs mostly in the southern half of the state.

Band-tailed pigeon. *Columba fasciata*. Page 148 photograph by Larry Ditto. Found in the high mountains of West Texas.

Common ground dove. *Columbina passerina*. Page 148 photograph by Ed Dutch. Usually found in South Texas; a winter visitor elsewhere in the state.

Wild turkey. *Meleagris gallopavo*. Pages 150, 152, and 153 photographs by Bill Reaves; page 151 photograph by Ed Dutch. The "king" of Texas game birds. Once found statewide, it is now restricted but has been reestablished in many areas through restocking.

Five-lined skink. *Eumeces fasciatus*. Page 154 photographs by John Tveten. Occurs in the eastern one-third of Texas.

Slender glass lizard. *Ophisaurus attenuatus*. Page 155 photograph by John Tveten. Legless, it may be distinguished from snakes by its ear openings and movable eyelids. Found in the eastern half of the state.

Greater earless lizard (Texas earless lizard). *Cophosaurus texanus*. Page 155 photograph by Reagan Bradshaw. Occurs in central and western Texas.

Green anole. *Anolis carolinensis*. Page 155 photograph by John Tveten; page 158 photograph by Reagan Bradshaw. Common in the eastern half of the state.

Ground skink. *Scincella laterale*. Page 156 photograph by John Tveten. Found in central and eastern Texas.

Collared lizard. *Crotaphytus collaris*. Page 156 photograph by Jim Whitcomb. Prefers rocky areas in central and western Texas.

Reticulated collared lizard. *Crotaphytus reticulatus*. Page 156 photograph by John Tveten. A protected species found only in the southwestern region of the state.

Tree lizard. *Urosaurus ornatus*. Page 157 photograph by Martin T. Fulfer. Occurs in the Edwards Plateau and Trans-Pecos Texas.

Small-mouthed salamander. *Ambystoma texanum*. Page 159 photograph by Reagan Bradshaw. Found in the eastern one-third of the state.

Whiptail. *Cnemidophorus* sp. Page 159 photograph by Martin T. Fulfer. Occurs statewide.

Mole salamander. *Ambystoma talpoideum*. Pages 160–161 photograph by J. F. Schultz. A protected species known only from Jasper and Nacogdoches counties.

Marbled salamander. *Ambystoma opacum*. Page 161 photograph by James C. Kroll. Found in far eastern Texas.

American alligator. *Alligator mississippiensis*. Page 162 *above*, photograph by Bill Duncan; *below*, photograph by Martin T. Fulfer; page 163 photograph by John Suhrstedt. Currently listed as an endangered species, it is increasing in some areas. Found in eastern Texas.

Speckled kingsnake. *Lampropeltis getulus*. Page 164 photograph by John Dyes. Common statewide.

Blotched water snake. *Nerodia erythrogaster*. Page 165 photograph by Perry Shankle, Jr.; page 166 photograph by Jim Whitcomb. Common statewide.

Western mud snake. *Farancia abacura*. Page 165 photograph by John Suhrstedt. Occurs in the eastern quarter of Texas.

Texas indigo snake. *Drymarchon corais*. Page 166 photograph by the *Texas Parks & Wildlife* staff. A protected species; occurs only in the southwesternmost region of the state.

Bullsnake. *Pituophis melanoleucus*. Page 166 photograph by Ron Perryman. A common snake throughout the state.

Trans-Pecos rat snake. *Elaphe subocularis*. Page 166 photograph by Frank Aguilar. Occurs in Trans-Pecos Texas.

Diamondback water snake. *Nerodia rhombifera*. Page 166 photograph by Neal Cook. Common in central and eastern Texas.

Coachwhip. *Masticophis flagellum*. Page 167 photograph by John Suhrstedt. Distributed statewide.

Eastern hognosed snake. *Heterodon platyrhinos*. Pages 168 and 169 *top* and *center*, photographs by James C. Kroll; page 169 *bottom*, photograph by John Dyes. Common in central and eastern Texas.

Rough green snake. *Opheodrys aestivus*. Page 170 photograph by Jim Whitcomb. Found in central and eastern Texas.

Black-necked garter snake. *Thamnophis cyrtopsis*. Page 171 photograph by Jim Whitcomb. From Trans-Pecos Texas and the Edwards Plateau.

Texas coral snake. *Micrurus fulvius*. Page 172 photograph by John Tveten. Poisonous; found in the eastern half of the state.

Western cottonmouth. *Agkistrodon piscivorus*. Page 173 photograph by John Tveten. Poisonous; occurs throughout central and eastern Texas near water.

Prairie kingsnake. *Lampropeltis calligaster*. Page 174 photograph by John Tveten. Occurs in the eastern half of Texas.

Copperhead. *Agkistrodon contortrix*. Page 175 photograph by John Tveten. Poisonous; found in the eastern three-fourths of the state.

Prairie rattlesnake. *Crotalus viridis*. Page 176 photograph by Bill Reaves. Poisonous; occurs in northwestern Texas and the Panhandle.

Western diamondback rattlesnake. *Crotalus atrox*. Page 177 photograph by Bill Reaves. Poisonous; from central and western Texas.

Northern gray tree frog. *Hyla versicolor*. Page 178 photograph by Neal Cook. Occurs in the eastern half of Texas.

Upland chorus frog. *Pseudacris triseriata*. Page 178 photograph by John Tveten. Found in the eastern one-third of Texas.

Texas cliff frog. *Syrrhophus marnocki*. Page 178 photograph by Leroy Williamson. From the Edwards Plateau.

Southern leopard frog. *Rana sphenocephala*. Page 178 photograph by John Tveten. Occurs statewide.

Giant toad. *Bufo marinus*. Page 178 photograph by John Tveten. A protected species from the extreme southern tip of the state.

Gulf Coast toad. *Bufo valliceps*. Page 178 photograph by John Tveten; page 180 photograph by Leroy Williamson. Found in the southern half of Texas.

Green tree frog. *Hyla cinerea*. Page 179 photograph by Terry Fischer. A species found in eastern Texas.

Spiny softshell turtle. *Trionyx spiniferus*. Page 180 photograph by John Tveten. Found in lakes and rivers throughout the state.

Texas tortoise. *Gopherus berlandieri*. Page 181 photograph by Bill Duncan. A protected species from southwestern Texas.

Red-eared turtle. *Chrysemys scripta*. Page 182 photograph by Martin T. Fulfer. Occurs throughout the state.

Common snapping turtle. *Chelydra serpentina*. Page 182 photograph by Richard Moree. Distributed throughout the state.

Eastern box turtle (three-toed box turtle). *Terrapene carolina*. Page 183 photograph by Jim Whitcomb. Occurs in the wooded eastern areas of Texas.

Western box turtle (ornate box turtle). *Terrapene ornata*. Page 184 photograph by Reagan Bradshaw. Common throughout the state.

River cooter (Texas slider). *Chrysemys concinna*. Page 185 photograph by Martin T. Fulfer. Found in central and eastern Texas.

Index

(Numbers in italics indicate pages of color plates.)